# Dropping In On...

# Boston

Brittany Canasi

rourkeeducationalmedia.com

*Scan for Related Titles
and Teacher Resources*

## Before Reading:

### Building Academic Vocabulary and Background Knowledge

Before reading a book, it is important to tap into what your child or students already know about the topic. This will help them develop their vocabulary, increase their reading comprehension, and make connections across the curriculum.

1.  Look at the cover of the book. What will this book be about?
2.  What do you already know about the topic?
3.  Let's study the Table of Contents. What will you learn about in the book's chapters?
4.  What would you like to learn about this topic? Do you think you might learn about it from this book? Why or why not?
5.  Use a reading journal to write about your knowledge of this topic. Record what you already know about the topic and what you hope to learn about the topic.
6.  Read the book.
7.  In your reading journal, record what you learned about the topic and your response to the book.
8.  After reading the book complete the activities below.

### Content Area Vocabulary
*Read the list. What do these words mean?*

annexing
famine
grim
heritage
historic
literature
protest
reenactments
slang
suburb

## After Reading:

### Comprehension and Extension Activity

After reading the book, work on the following questions with your child or students in order to check their level of reading comprehension and content mastery.

1.  What is Boston best known for? (Summarize)
2.  What makes the city such a popular place to visit? (Infer)
3.  What influential people in U.S. history lived there? (Asking questions)
4.  What do you think is the most interesting thing about Boston? (Text to self connection)
5.  Why did city leaders fill in Boston's marshy areas? (Asking questions)

### Extension Activity

Create a travel brochure about Boston. Include several places visitors should see. Write short, exciting paragraphs that highlight the most interesting things about the city. And don't forget to add pictures! You can draw them or print them out from the Internet.

# Table of Contents

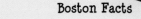

Old as the Hills ..................... 4

Famous Bostonians .............. 10

The Freedom Trail ................. 14

Year-Round Playground ........ 18

Sports in the City ................. 22

Delicious Diversity ............... 26

Timeline .............................. 29

Glossary ............................. 30

Index................................... 31

Show What You Know........... 31

Websites to Visit ................. 31

About the Author ................. 32

## Boston Facts

**Founded:** 1630
**Land area:** 48.28 square miles (77.7 square kilometers)
**Elevation:** 141 feet (43 meters)
**Previous name:** Trimountaine

**Population:** 655,884
**Average Daytime Temperatures:**
**winter:** 42 degrees Fahrenheit (5.6 degrees Celsius)
**spring:** 67 degrees Fahrenheit (19.4 degrees Celsius)
**summer:** 82 degrees Fahrenheit (27.8 degrees Celsius)
**fall:** 73 degrees Fahrenheit (22.8 degrees Celsius)

**Ethnic Diversity:**
White, non-Hispanic 53.9%
Black/African-American 24.4%
American Indian/Alaska Native 0.4%
Asian 8.9%
Hispanic/Latino 17.5%

**City Nickname:** Beantown

**Number of Annual Visitors:** 16,250,000

United States

NH
VT
Boston, MA
NY
RI
CT

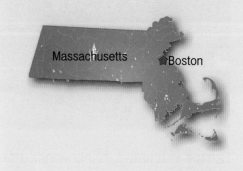

Massachusetts    Boston

# Old as the Hills

Boston, the capital of Massachusetts, is one of the oldest cities in the United States. It was founded in 1630. Its history includes a lot of notable firsts for the nation.

Boston is located in the northeastern United States on Massachusetts Bay, part of the Atlantic Ocean.

The Tremont Street Subway was at the center of the first subway line in Boston. It's now a historical landmark!

America's first subway system was built in Boston. It opened in 1897. The city's streets were bustling with traffic even back then. The subway was designed to remove the streetcar lines from the streets and make way for cars.

Many tunnels had flying junctions in them, or ways to safely have more than one train pass through.

The first American public school, the Boston Latin School, opened in Boston in 1635. It still welcomes students today.

**Boston Notes**

When settlers first moved to Boston, they called it Trimountaine, after the three large hills that were there. They later changed it to Boston, since many important settlers at the time came from Boston, Lincolnshire, England.

Every student who attends the school has to learn Latin for at least three years.

Harvard University was the first university in the United States. It was founded one year after Boston Latin School, in 1636.

The first public park was created in Boston in 1634. It's called Boston Common. It used to be a place for people's cows to graze.

Harvard has two crew, or rowing teams: lightweight and heavyweight. The lightweight team requires men to weigh less that 160 pounds and women less than 130 pounds.

Swan boat tours have been happening in Boston Common since 1877, and the same family has owned the boats since the beginning.

Boston isn't just old, it's big! At 89.63 square miles (232.14 square kilometers), it's Massachusetts's largest city.

But it wasn't always that size. Boston has nearly tripled in size since it was founded. Part of Boston's growth came from **annexing**, or adding, nearby towns.

Trinity Church was built on wet marshland that had been filled in. To keep the building from sinking, the foundation is made up of wood, cement, and four large granite pyramids.

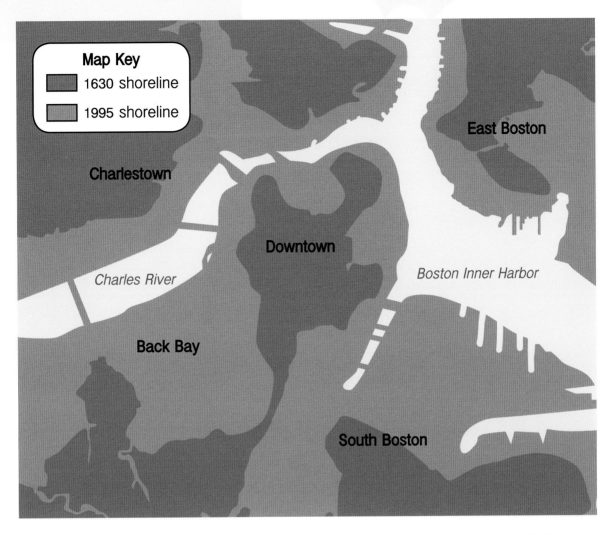

**Map Key**
- 1630 shoreline
- 1995 shoreline

Charlestown

East Boston

Downtown

Charles River

Boston Inner Harbor

Back Bay

South Boston

A lot of the land used to fill in marshes was taken from the city's large hills. Today, there isn't much left of them, and the city is mostly flat.

Boston also expanded when city leaders decided to fill its coastal inlets and mudflats with dirt to turn the areas into useable land. The landfill projects started in 1820 and continued through the early 1900s.

Dirt from nearby hills was brought in to fill the marshy areas. And after the Great Boston Fire in 1872, debris from destroyed buildings was used to fill in more areas.

# Famous Bostonians

Benjamin Franklin was born in Boston in 1706. Many of his inventions helped people. He invented bifocals so people could see far away and up close with the same glasses. He invented the Franklin Stove, which provided heat for homes.

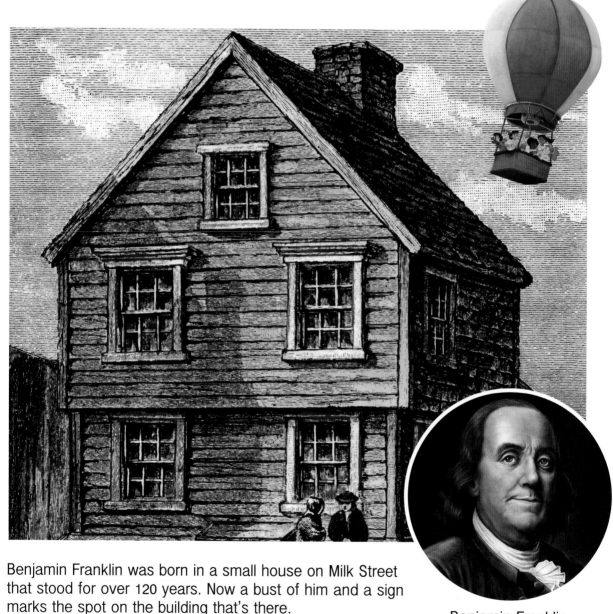

Benjamin Franklin was born in a small house on Milk Street that stood for over 120 years. Now a bust of him and a sign marks the spot on the building that's there.

Benjamin Franklin
(1706–1790)

Paul Revere
(1735–1818)

Like Ben, Paul knew how to do a lot of things. He was a silversmith, an engraver, and a dentist. Imagine going to your dentist and also buying a necklace and flower vase!

Paul Revere is an important person in American history. Born in Boston in 1734, he became a spy during the Revolutionary War (1775–1783). He is known for his famous horseback ride to warn two Patriots that they were about to be arrested by the British. On his way, he and other men warned many people about the British invasion.

Edgar Allan Poe (1809–1849), a famous author, was born in Boston. He was the first person to write about detectives. He wrote a lot of short stories that were **grim** and mysterious.

A lot of United States presidents have called Boston home. John Adams was the second president of the United States. His son, John Quincy Adams, became the sixth president. John F. Kennedy (JFK) was in both the U.S. House of Representatives and the Senate before becoming a U.S. president. George H. W. Bush was born just outside of Boston and was both a vice president and president of the United States.

John Adams
(President from 1797–1801)

John Quincy Adams
(President from 1825–1829)

John F. Kennedy
(President from 1961–1963)

George H. W. Bush
(President from 1989–1993)

John Adams had a very important signature. He was the second consecutive president to have his signature on the Declaration of Independence.

# The Freedom Trail

The Freedom Trail is a must-visit site in Boston. It's actually 16 different places all connected by a two and a half mile (4.02 kilometer) brick road. The Old South Meeting House, located on the trail, is the church where everyone met before the Boston Tea Party, a political **protest**. It was the largest building in Boston at the time. It's a good thing it was, too, because more than 5,000 people showed up that day!

### Boston Notes

The Boston Tea Party in 1773 was a protest on taxes to the King of England. It took place just before the Revolutionary War. Protesters dumped all the tea that was on three large ships into Boston Harbor.

If a fire engine hadn't arrived just in time, the Old South Meeting House would have been destroyed in the Great Boston Fire of 1872.

The Old Corner Bookstore, built in 1718, was the center of Boston **literature**. It published books from some of the most famous authors in U.S. history, including Harriet Beecher Stowe, Nathaniel Hawthorne, and Louisa May Alcott. In 1960, it was almost torn down to make room for a parking garage. Luckily, the city raised money to save it. It's now a protected **historic** site.

If you want to find a good book these days, you'll have to look elsewhere. A fast food restaurant now operates in the building.

To protect the Paul Revere House from being demolished, John P. Reynolds, Jr. purchased it in 1904. He was Paul Revere's great-grandson.

The Paul Revere House is the oldest building in downtown Boston. It's also the only house on the Freedom Trail. Paul Revere lived there when he made his famous ride in 1775.

The Granary Burying Ground is named after the giant grain storage facility that used to be next to it. It has a lot of famous people buried there, such as Benjamin Franklin's parents, John Hancock, and Paul Revere.

On the Freedom Trail, you can also find the *USS Constitution*, a ship used in the War of 1812. It's the world's oldest commissioned warship. It was nicknamed "Old Ironsides" because cannonballs seemed to bounce right off it.

The *USS Constitution* is made of three layers of wood. The copper parts were made by Paul Revere.

**Boston Notes**

Cows used to take care of cutting the grass at the Granary Burying Ground. The grave markers were organized in the 1800s so a new invention—the lawnmower—could be used to cut the grass.

# Year-Round Playground

With more than 60 historic sites, thousands of restaurants, and hundreds of hotels, Boston is one of the top cities for tourism in the United States. It is also considered one of the most economically powerful cities in the world. It has the sixth largest economy in the U.S. and the twelfth largest worldwide.

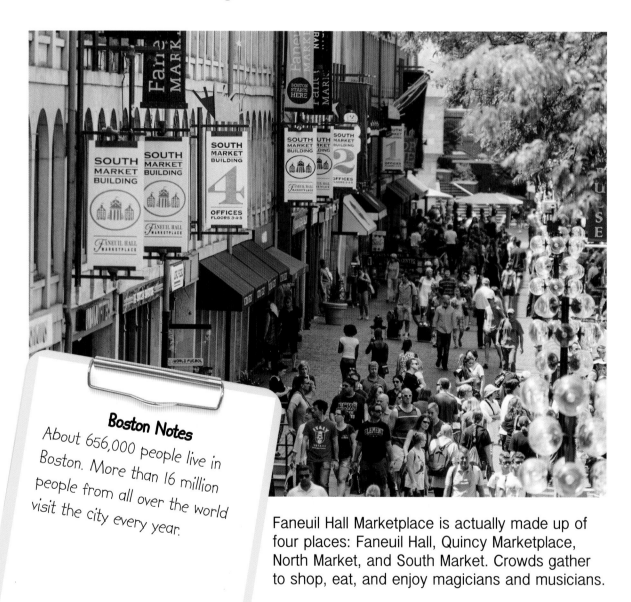

**Boston Notes**
About 656,000 people live in Boston. More than 16 million people from all over the world visit the city every year.

Faneuil Hall Marketplace is actually made up of four places: Faneuil Hall, Quincy Marketplace, North Market, and South Market. Crowds gather to shop, eat, and enjoy magicians and musicians.

# Music and More

Many famous bands got their start in Boston, including Aerosmith and The Mighty Mighty Bosstones.

The Boston Symphony Orchestra is one of the top five orchestras in the United States. They perform at Symphony Hall. In the Hall, there are stone plaques that line the walls, but they're almost all blank. There is only one with a famous composer's name: Ludwig van Beethoven (1770–1827).

IF YOU AND 2,624 OF YOUR CLOSEST FRIENDS WANTED TO RENT OUT SYMPHONY HALL, IT WOULD ONLY COST EACH OF YOU $2.59.

The Greek and Roman statues set into the walls of Symphony Hall all have something to do with music or art.

Boston has many festivals throughout the year. First Night takes place from New Year's Eve to New Year's Day. About 1.5 million people come for the art, music, parades, and midnight fireworks.

Harborfest takes place in the days leading up to the Fourth of July. It celebrates American independence and Boston's history. They also have war **reenactments** from the Revolutionary War.

First Night traditions also include ice skating on Frog Pond, light displays, and ice sculptures.

The St. Patrick's Day Parade features bagpipes, marching bands, decorated floats, entertainers, and tons of other participants.

South Boston hosts one of the biggest St. Patrick's Day parades in the United States. The parade is a celebration of Irish **heritage**. People from all over the country come to Boston to perform in it.

# Sports in the City

Boston has teams in all four major leagues: baseball, football, hockey, and basketball. It is one of only six cities in the country that has won championships in every sport.

The Boston Red Sox was one of the first professional baseball teams. They play in Fenway Park, the oldest baseball stadium that's still in use in the United States.

Fenway Park hosted its first professional baseball game on April 20, 1912.

Until recently, Bostonians thought they were under "The Curse of the Bambino." In 1920, they traded a famous player named Babe Ruth to the New York Yankees. They didn't win another World Series for 86 years, and the Yankees won their first World Series the first year Babe Ruth played for them.

### The First World Series

Before Fenway was built, Boston hosted the first World Series championship game in 1903 at the Huntington Avenue Grounds. The Boston Americans of the American League beat the Pittsburg Pirates, five games to three.

Babe Ruth
(1895–1948)

Babe Ruth was one of the first five people inducted into the Baseball Hall of Fame.

The Boston Celtics basketball team and Boston Bruins hockey team play at TD Garden, an indoor sports arena. For basketball games, they cover the ice with a court.

The New England Patriots are Boston's professional football team. They used to be called the Boston Patriots, but they moved to a new stadium in a **suburb** of Boston.

Larry Bird is a famous Boston Celtics player. He was part of the 1992 Olympics "Dream Team."

About 500,000 people stand on the streets to cheer for the Boston Marathon runners each year.

The Boston Marathon is one of the most well-known events in the city. It's been a tradition for more than 100 years. Only 18 people ran the first Boston Marathon in 1897. Now, more than 30,000 runners from around the world compete in it.

# Delicious Diversity

Boston's residents come from diverse backgrounds, so the city is a great place to find Chinese, Italian, Japanese, Irish, or Jamaican food.

In the mid-1800s, many people moved to Boston from Ireland because of a potato **famine**. Now, more Irish people live in Boston than any major city in the United States.

In honor of the 150th anniversary of the Irish Famine, a memorial park was created in downtown Boston in 1998. It is part of the Freedom Trail.

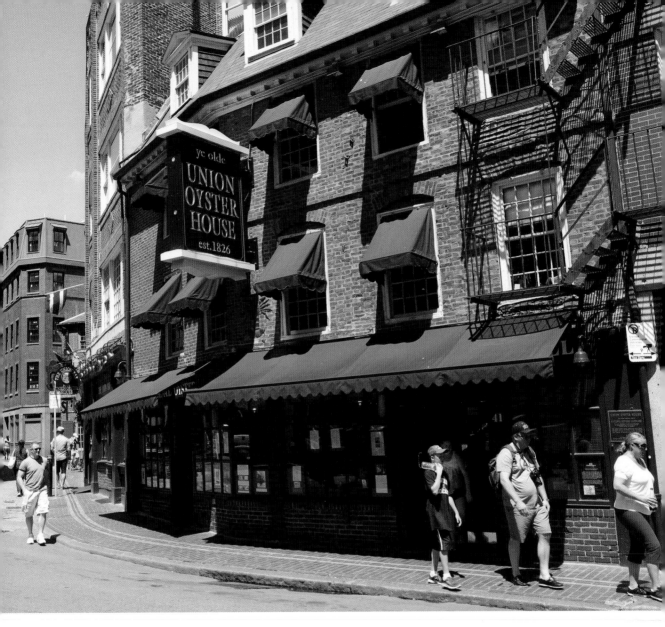

Union Oyster House on Union Street is the oldest continuously operating restaurant in the United States.

In the North End neighborhood, you'll find Italian food, such as cheesy ravioli, calamari, and cannoli. There are also many street festivals throughout the year.

Boston has a long history of fishing and farming, so local dishes often include seafood and dairy. Some popular dishes are fish and chips, lobster, fried clams, and New England clam chowder.

# Outdoor Fun

In the summer, Bostonians love to be outdoors. You can check out a farmer's market and pick up some fresh fruit, or rent a kayak and make your way down the Charles River. Want to stay cool? Hop on the T, Boston's subway, and check out the sea life at the New England Aquarium.

Boston gets about 44 inches (111 centimeters) of snow every year. There's still plenty to do when the temperatures drop! You can ice skate on Frog Pond in Boston Common, or watch a figure skating show. The Skating Spectacular is performed the same night the Christmas tree is lit in Boston Common.

## Speak Like a Bostonian

Boston locals use a lot of **slang**. Sometimes it sounds like Bostonians have their own language! Here are a few slang words and their definitions:

- *Beantown*-nickname for the City of Boston
- *bubbler*-water fountain
- *carriage*-shopping cart
- *frappe*-milkshake
- *jimmies*-sprinkles
- *wicked*-another word for "cool" or "very"

# Timeline

**1630**
Boston is founded by English Puritans.

**1636**
America's first college, Harvard University, opens.

**1690**
The first American newspaper, *The Boston News-Letter*, is published.

**1729**
The Old South Meeting House is built.

**1773**
The Boston Tea Party occurs.

**1822**
Boston officially becomes a city.

**1872**
The Great Fire breaks out, destroying much of the city. It's still considered one of the most costly fires in American history.

**1903**
The first World Series is held in Boston. The Boston Americans of the American League beat the Pittsburg Pirates, five games to three.

**1993**
The John F. Kennedy Library and Museum opens in Boston.

**2013**
Boston Marathon bombing kills three people and injures more than 260 others.

**1631**
The first ship built in America sets sail from Boston.

**1676**
The first coffeehouse opens in Boston.

**1706**
Benjamin Franklin is born in Boston.

**1770**
The Boston Massacre, a street fight between colonists and British soldiers, takes place.

**1776**
British forces retreat from Boston.

**1852**
The Boston Public Library is established.

**1897**
The first subway system in the U.S. opens in Boston.

**1912**
Fenway Park opens.

**2012**
Boston's population reaches 636,000.

# Glossary

**annexing** (AN-eks-een): taking control of a country or territory by force

**famine** (FAM-in): a serious lack of food in a geographic area

**grim** (grim): very serious or forbidding

**heritage** (HER-i-tij): traditions and beliefs that a country or society consider an important part of its history

**historic** (hi-STOR-ik): famous or important in history

**literature** (LIT-ur-uh-chur): written works that have lasting value or interest

**protest** (PROH-test): a demonstration or statement against something

**reenactments** (ree-uhn-ACT-muhnts): events that act out a past event

**slang** (slang): colorful or lively words and phrases used in ordinary conversation but not in formal speech or writing

**suburb** (SUHB-urb): an area or a district on or close to the outer edge of a city

# Index

Adams, John  12, 13

Boston Common  7, 28

Boston Tea Party  14, 29

Franklin, Benjamin  10, 16, 29

Great Boston Fire  9, 14, 29

Irish  21, 26

North End  27

Old Corner Bookstore  15

Revere, Paul  11, 16, 17

Revolutionary War  11, 14, 20

Ruth, Babe  23

Trimountaine  6

*USS Constitution*  17

# Show What You Know

1. Why did Irish families begin coming to the United States?

2. Why did the Boston Patriots change their name to the New England Patriots?

3. Why was the Old Corner Bookstore so important to American literature?

4. What were some of the things that Benjamin Franklin invented?

5. What were the two ways Boston expanded its size?

# Websites to Visit

www.jfklibrary.org

www.thefreedomtrail.org

www.americaslibrary.gov/aa/franklinb/aa_franklinb_subj.html

# About the Author

Brittany Canasi's job is in television, and her passion is in writing. She has a B.A. in Creative Writing from Florida State University. She loves to travel to new places and learn about new cultures, her favorite place being London. More than anything, she loves to try new food, especially if it's dessert. She lives in Los Angeles with her fiancé and very scruffy dog.

**Meet The Author!**
www.meetREMauthors.com

PHOTO CREDITS: Cover © janniswerner; United States Air Force/Wikipedia, Marcio Silva, Gregobagel; page 4 © ShoreTie; page 5 © Niday Picture Library/Alamy Stock Photo, Boston Transit Commision/ Wikipedia; page 6 © Svetlana Milijkovi/Wikipedia; page 7 © Marcio Silva; page 8 © Shunyu Fan; page 10 © Northwind Picture Archives/Alamy Stock Photo, JOE CICAK; page 11 © Sean Pavone; page 12 © Wynnter, Cecil Stoughton, Wikipedia; page 13 © tran=veler1116; page 14 © F11photo; page 15 © Clarence Holmes Photography/Alamy Stock Photo; page 16 © Ken Wiedermann; page 17 © Shananies; page 18 © helenecanada; page 19 © Americanspirit; page 20 ©  CO Leong; page 21 © Liviu Toader; page 22 © Joyce Vincent; page 23 ©  Wikipedia; page 24 © Jerry Coli; page 25 © Marcio Silva; page 26 © Ingfbruno; page 27 © stelya; page 29 © Jorge Salcedo, Marcio Silva, JOE CICAK, Joyce Vincent

Edited by: Keli Sipperley

Illustrations by: Caroline Romanet

Cover and interior design by: Jen Thomas

**Library of Congress PCN Data**

Dropping in on Boston / Brittany Canasi
ISBN 978-1-68191-408-4 (hard cover)
ISBN 978-1-68191-450-3 (soft cover)
ISBN 978-1-68191-488-6 (e-Book)
Library of Congress Control Number: 2015951574

Printed in the United States of America, North Mankato, Minnesota

**Also Available as:**

ROURKE'S
e-Books